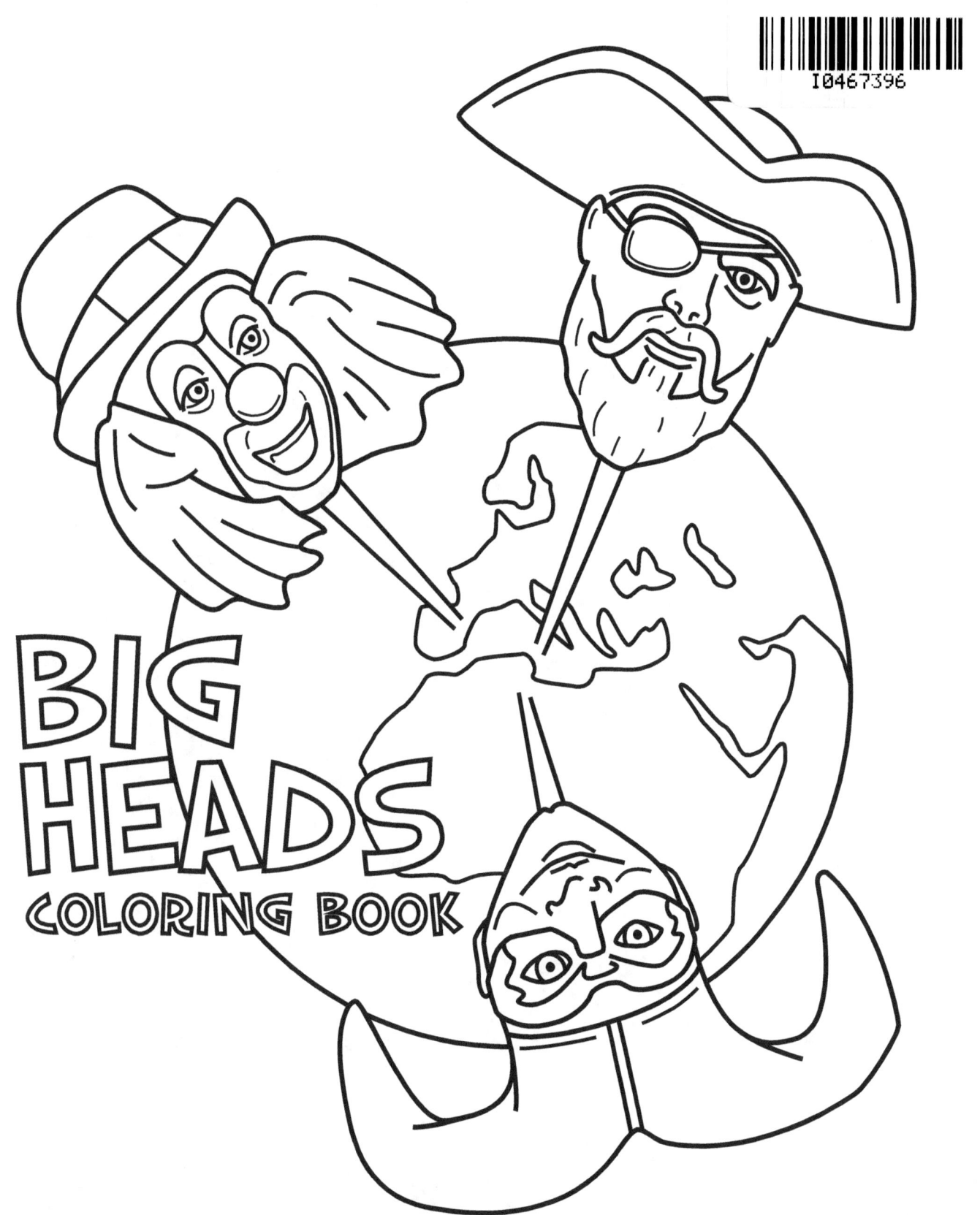

BIG
HEADS
COLORING BOOK

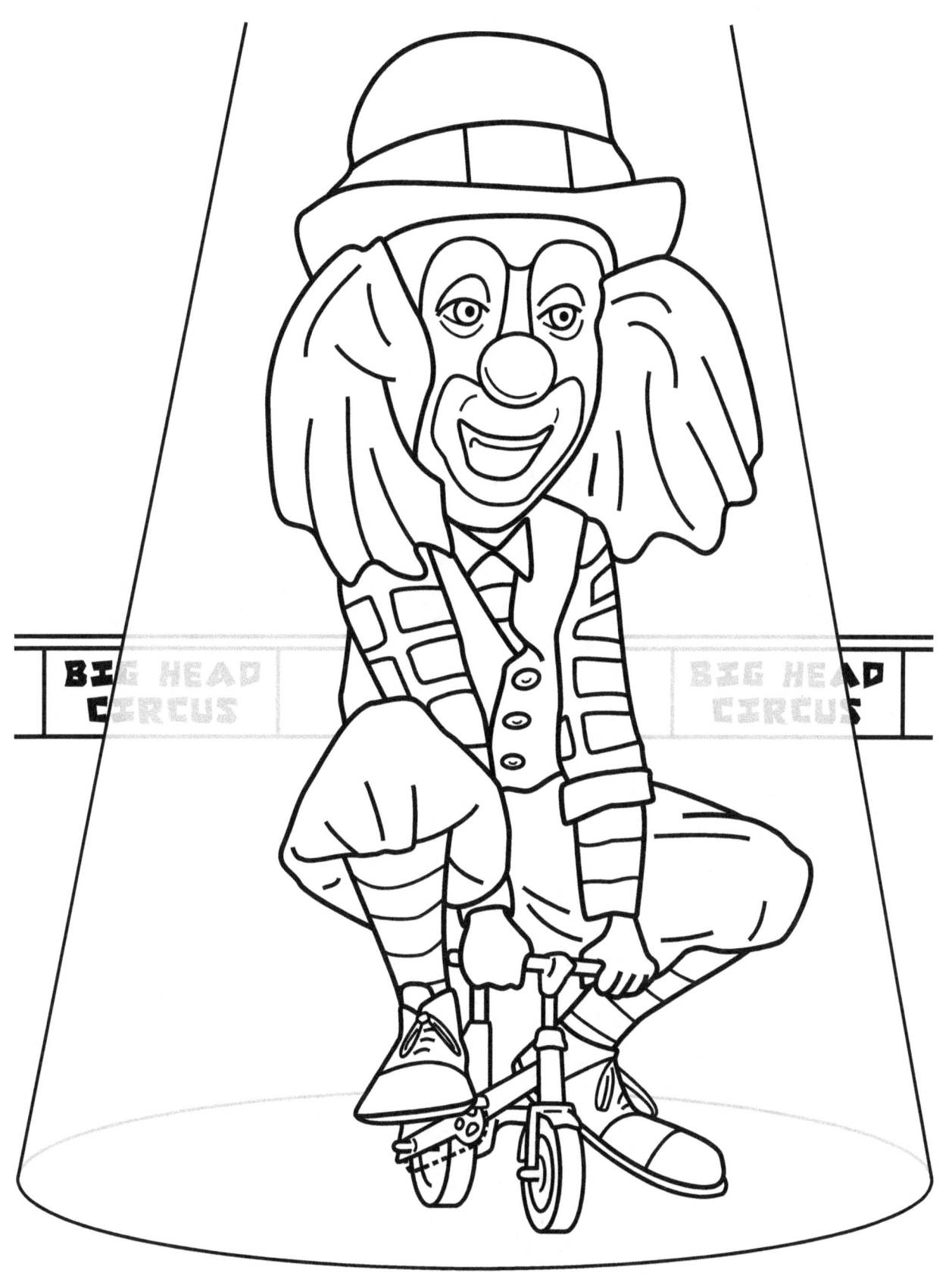

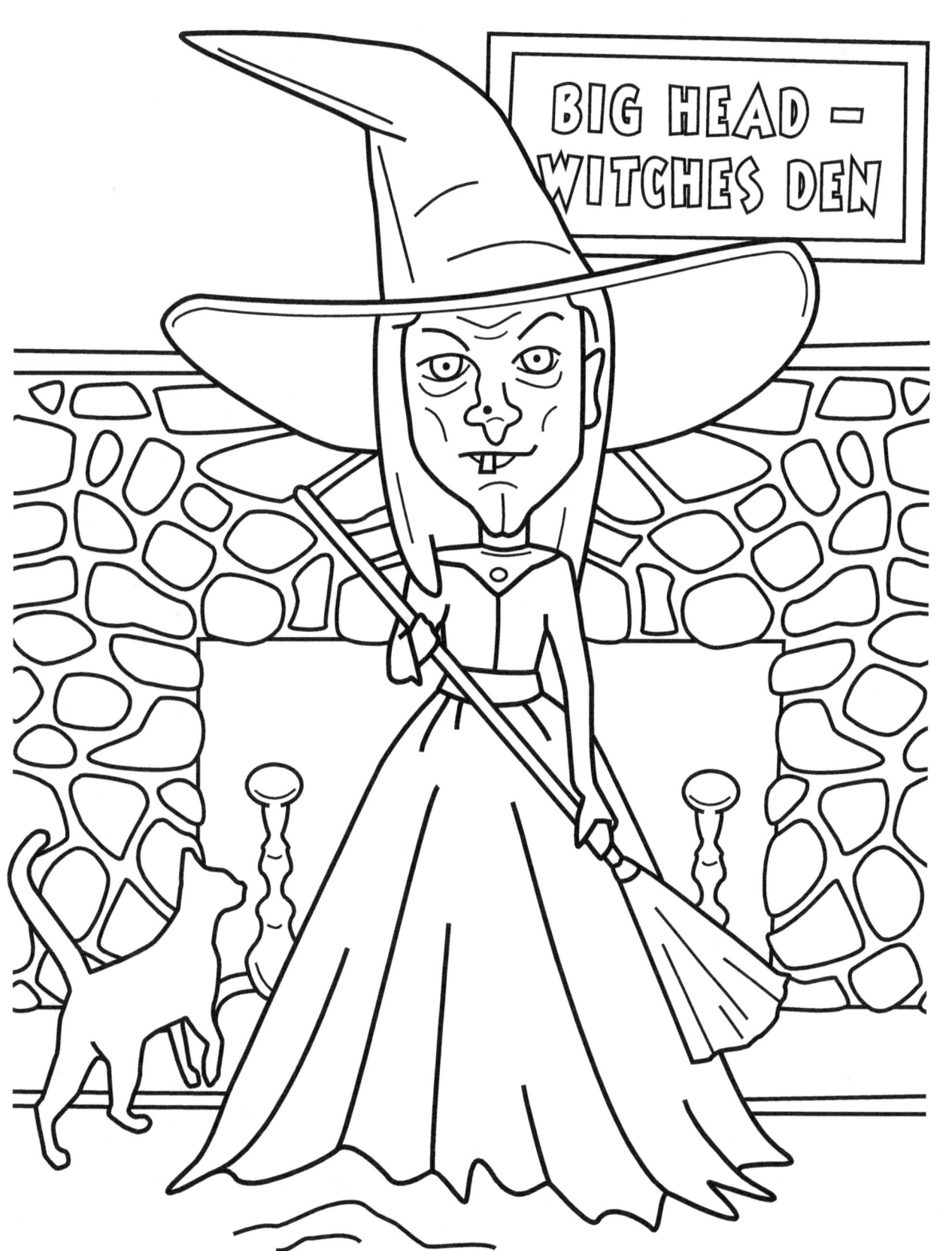

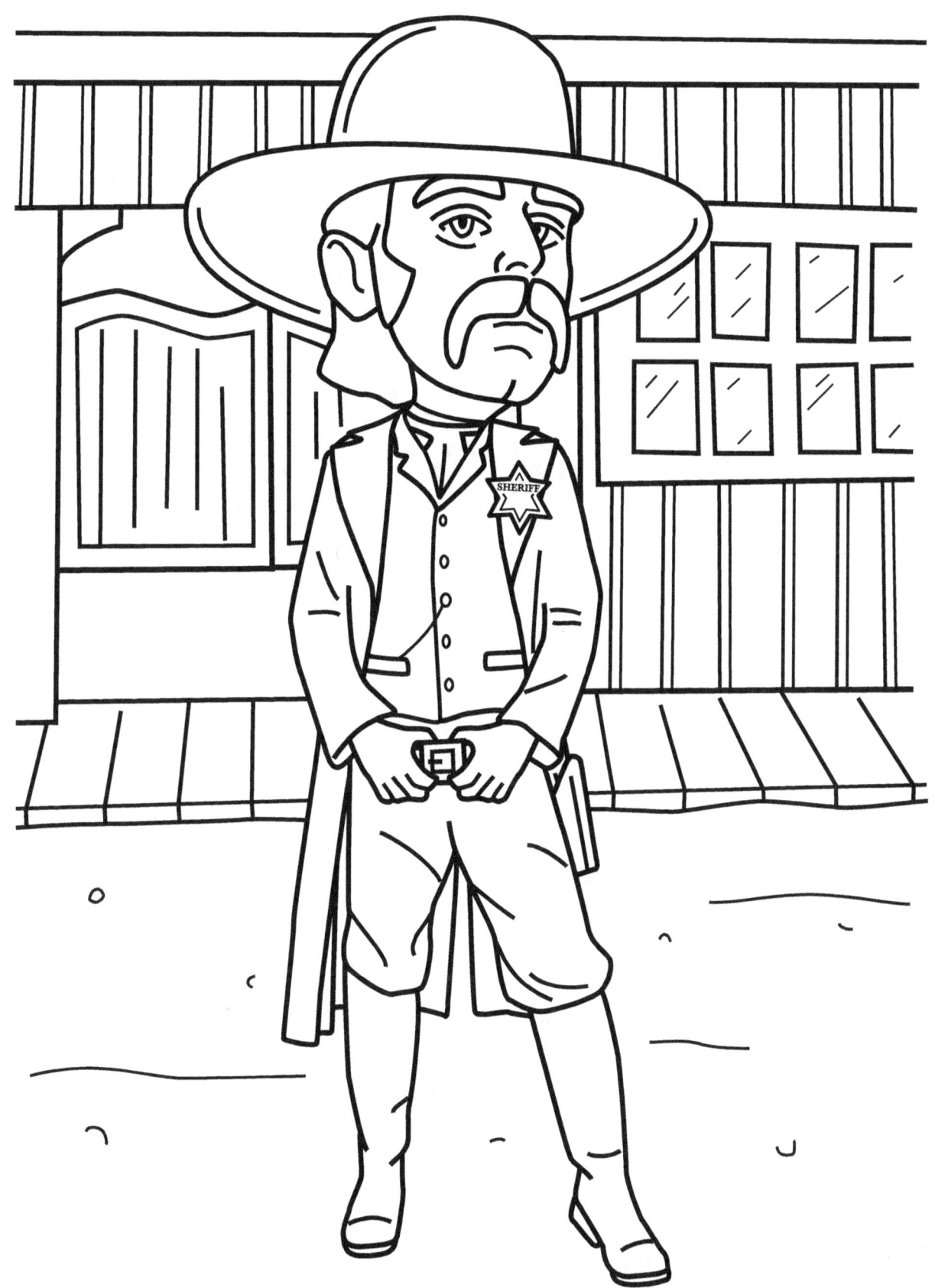

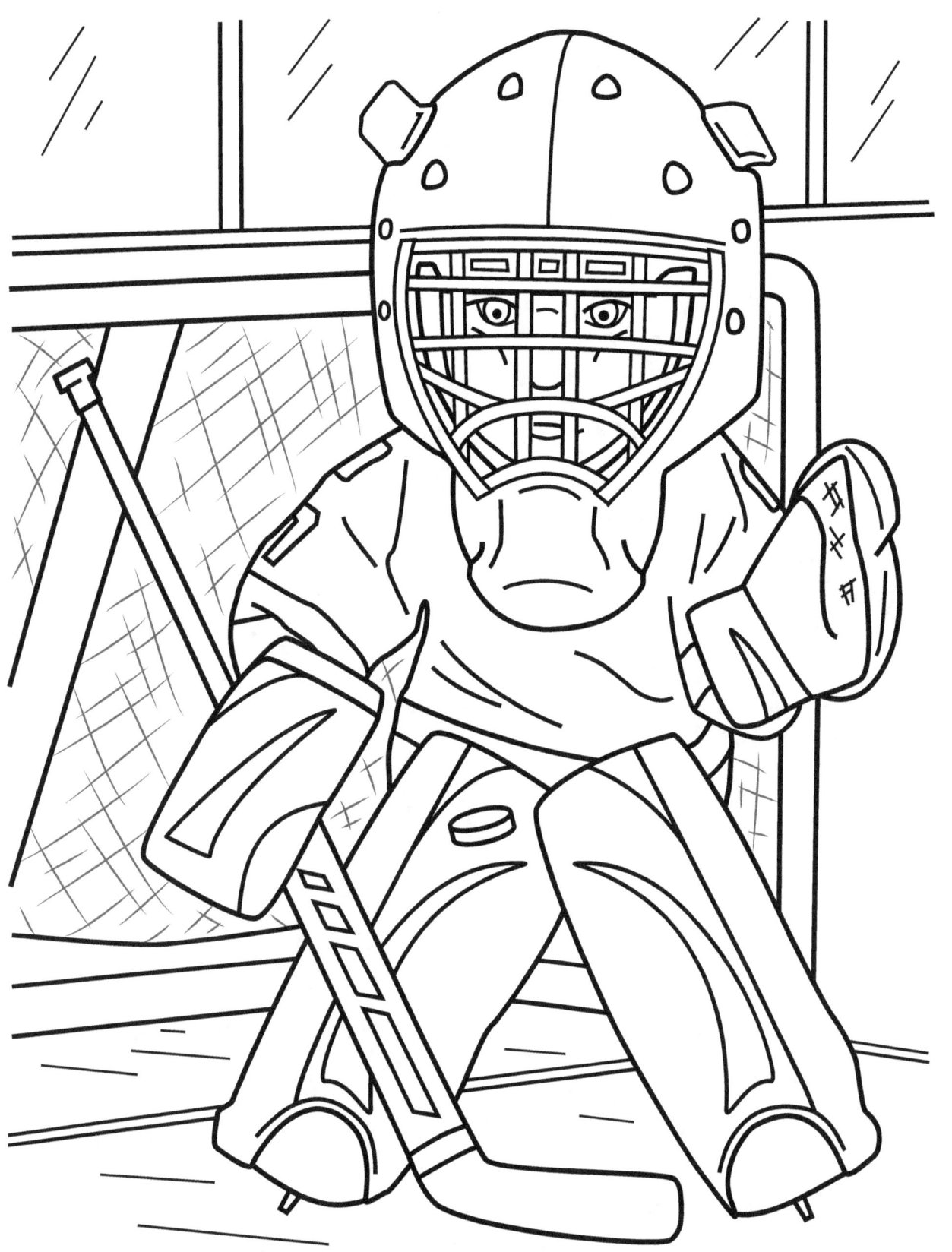

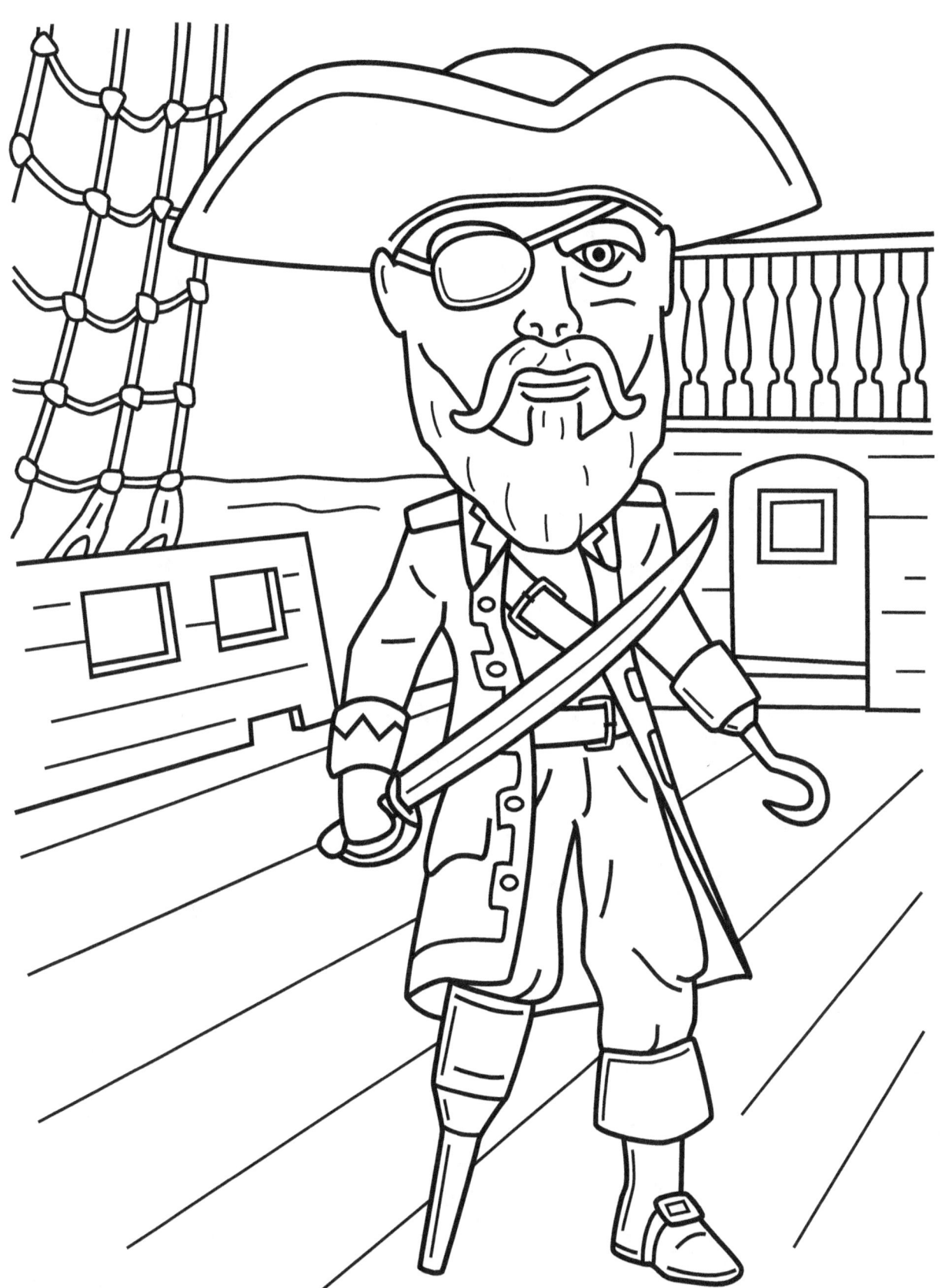

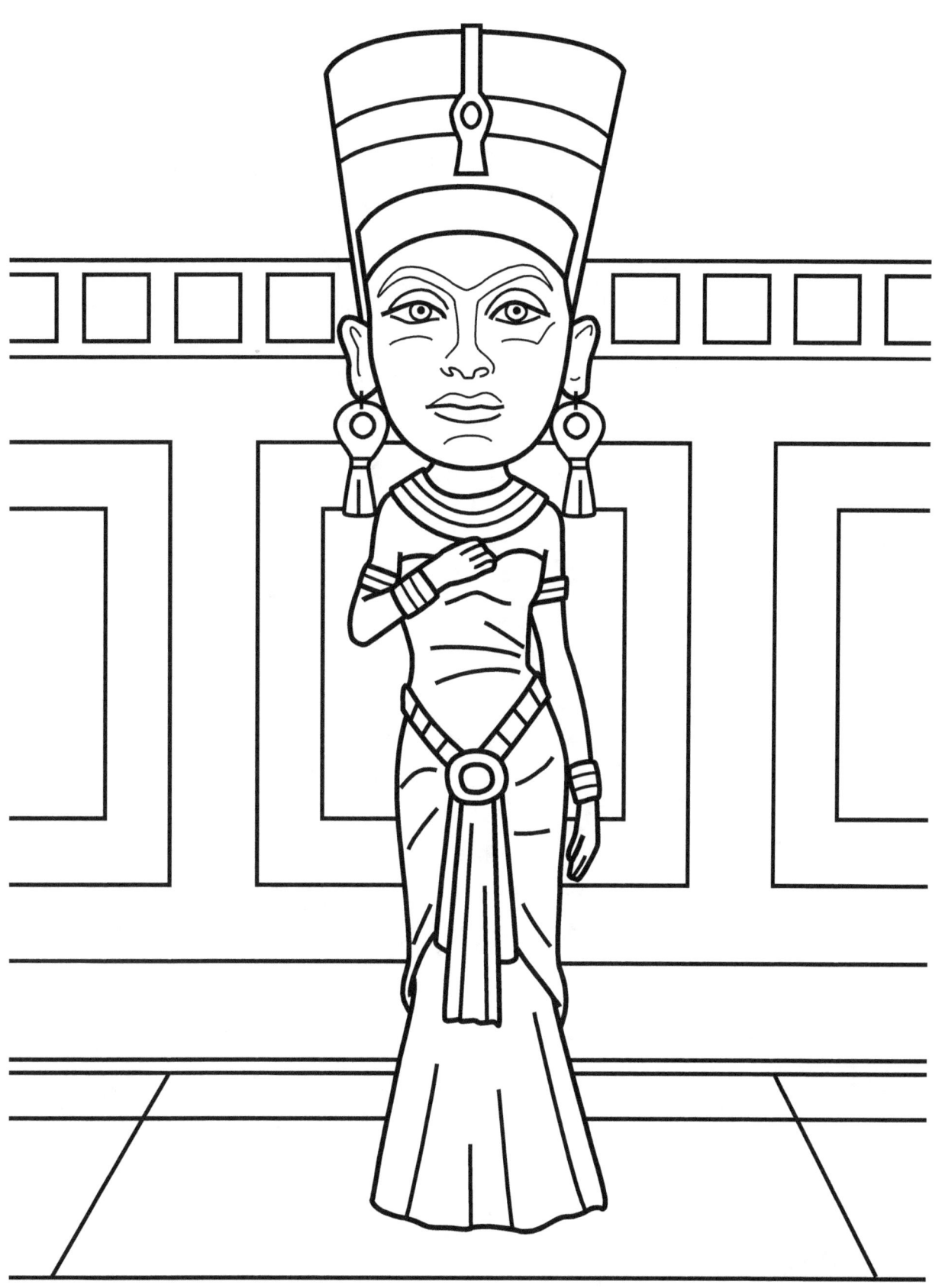

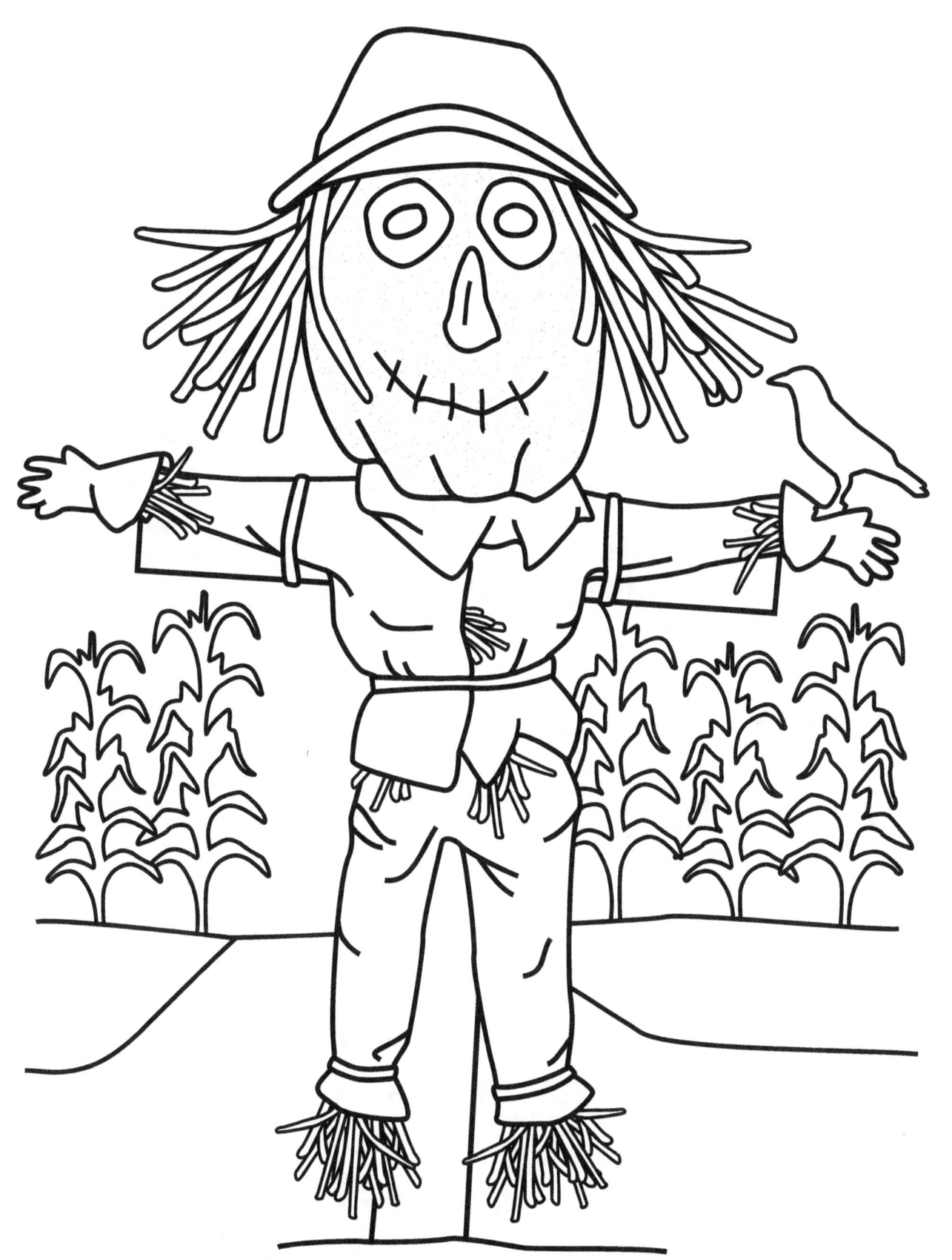

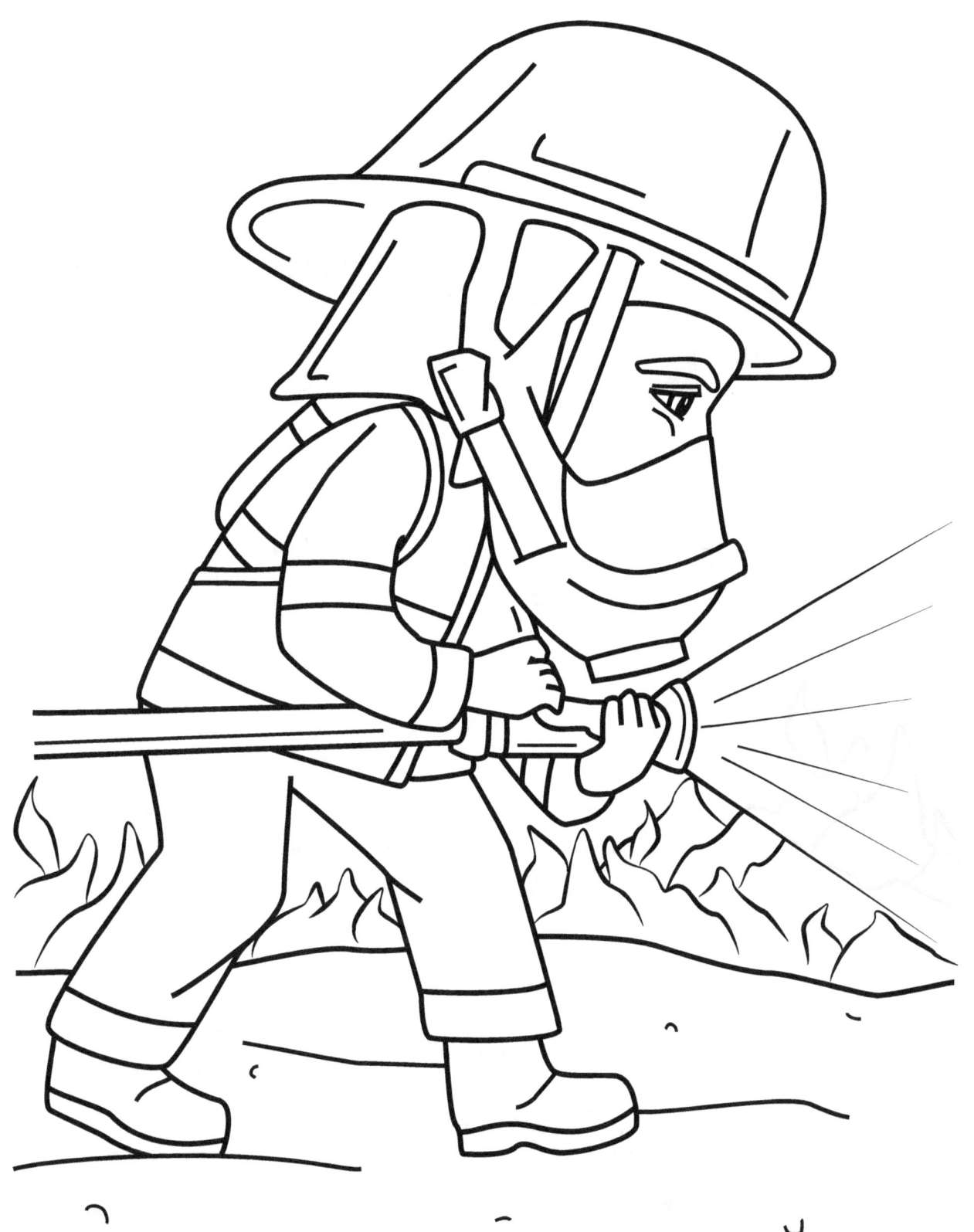

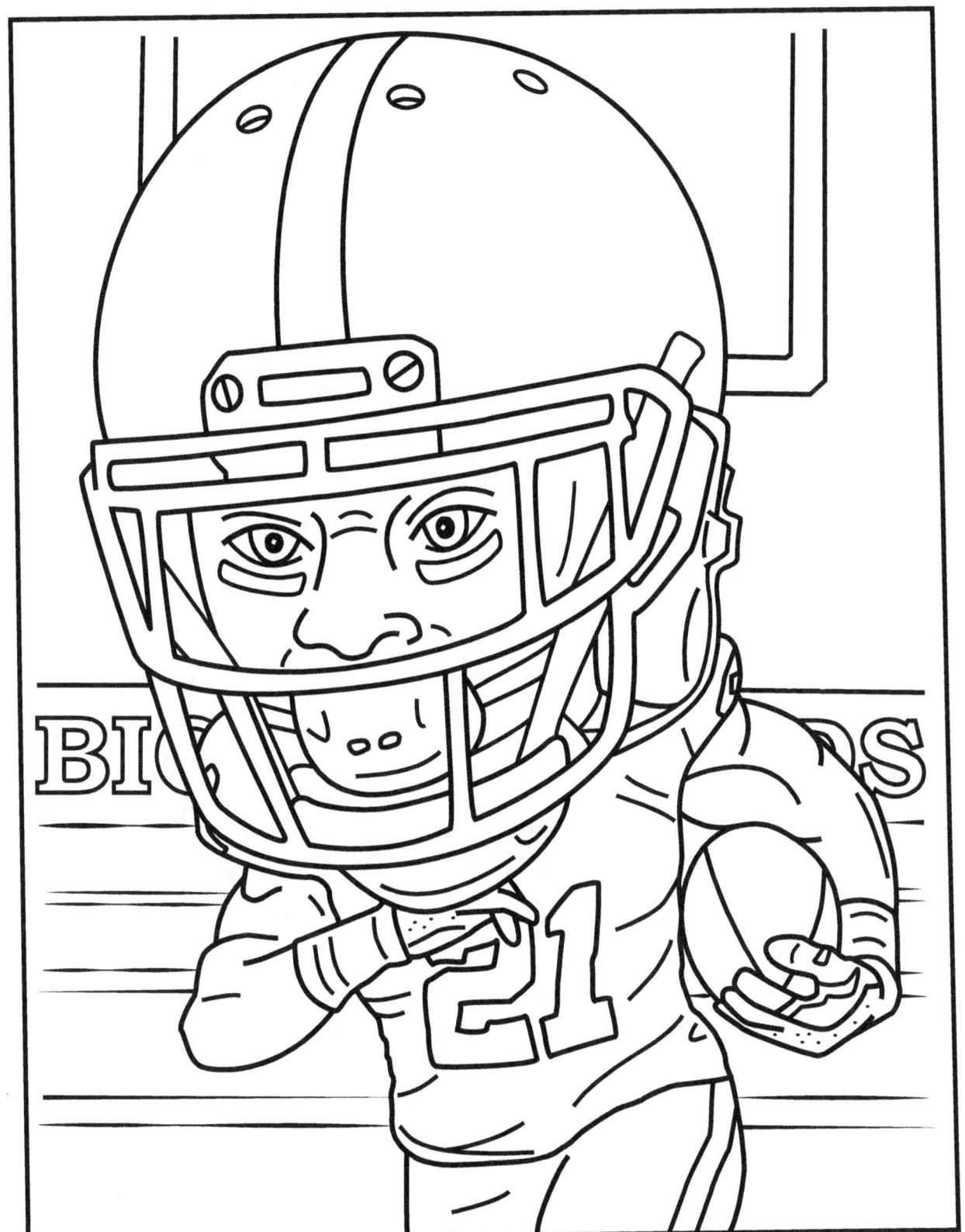

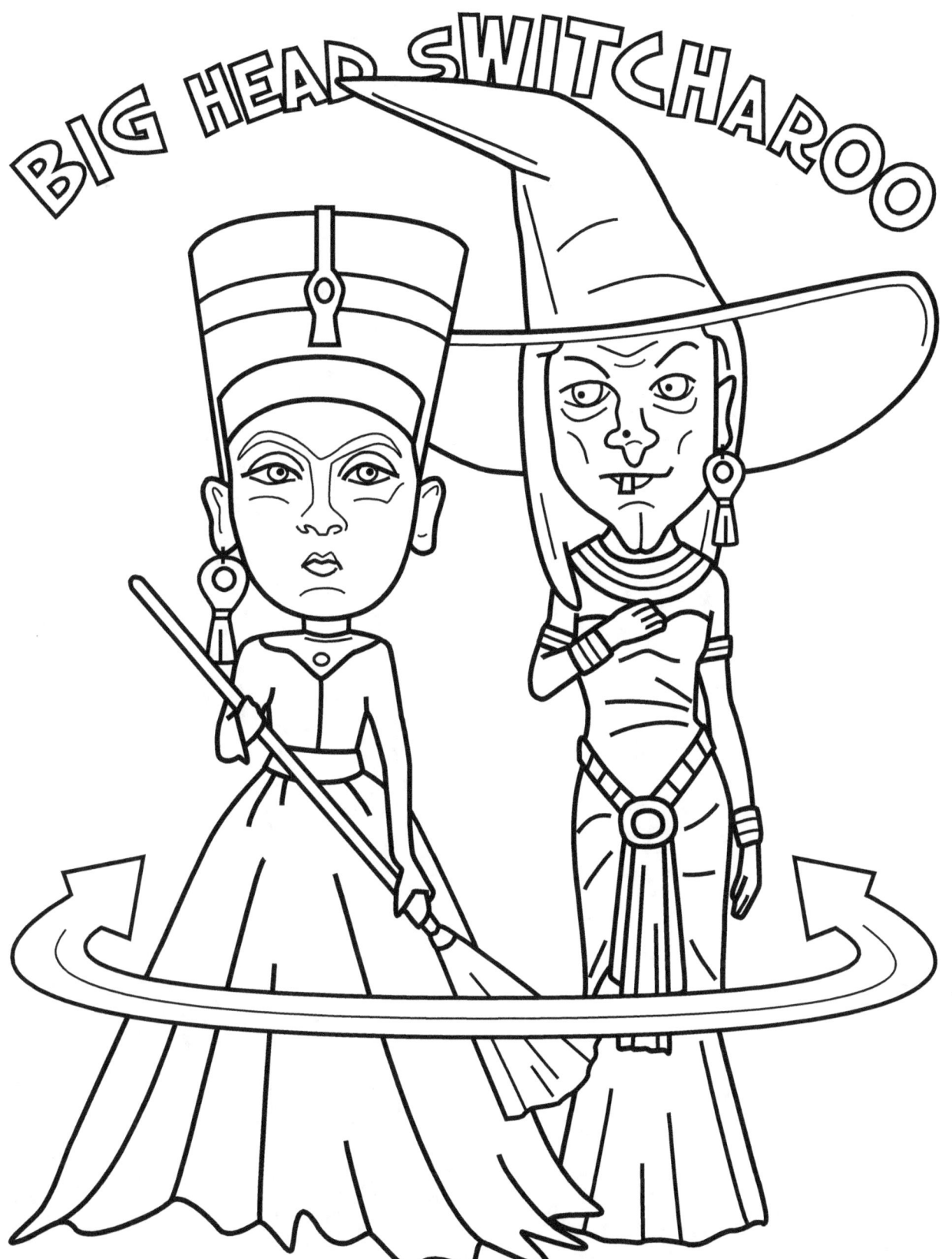

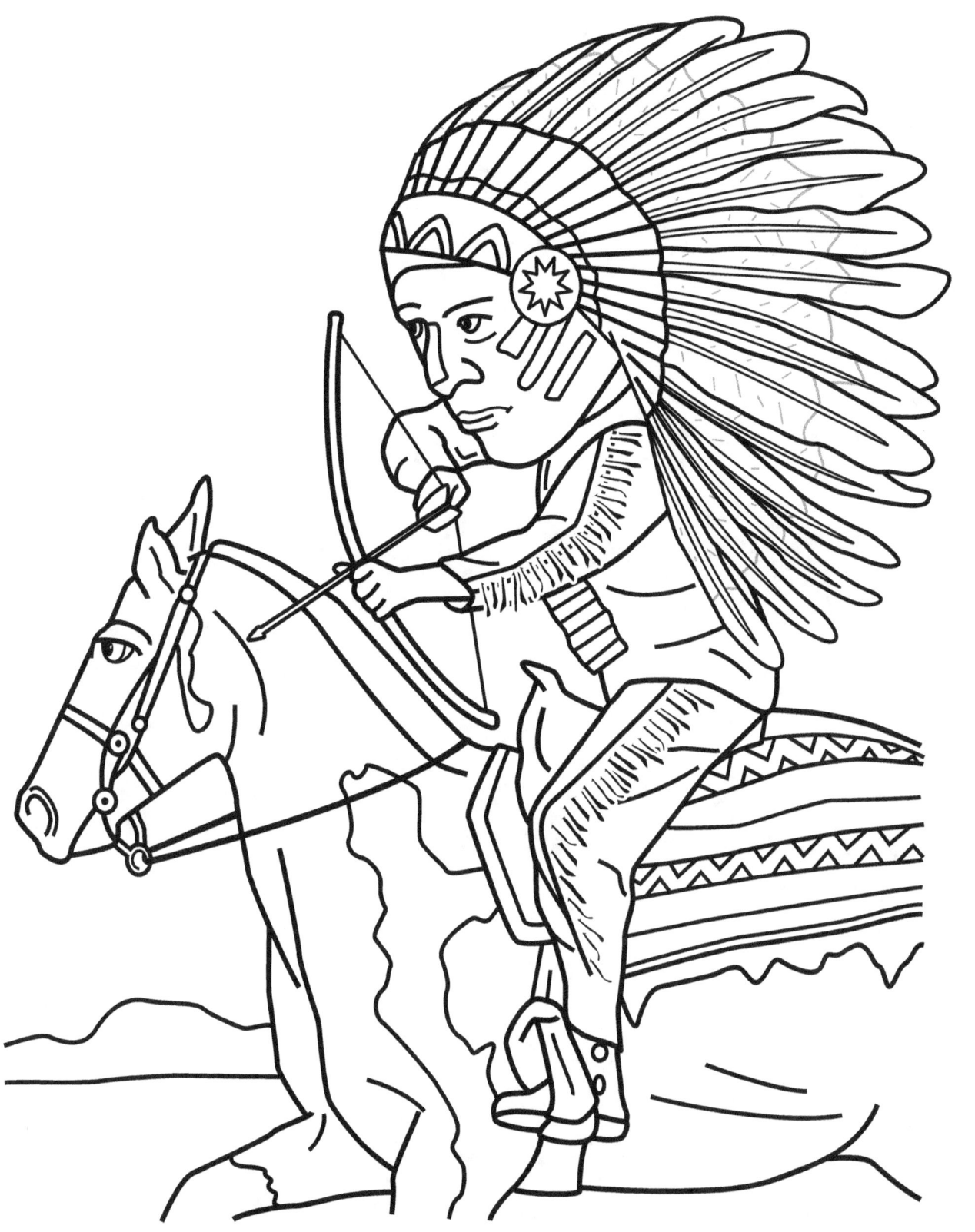

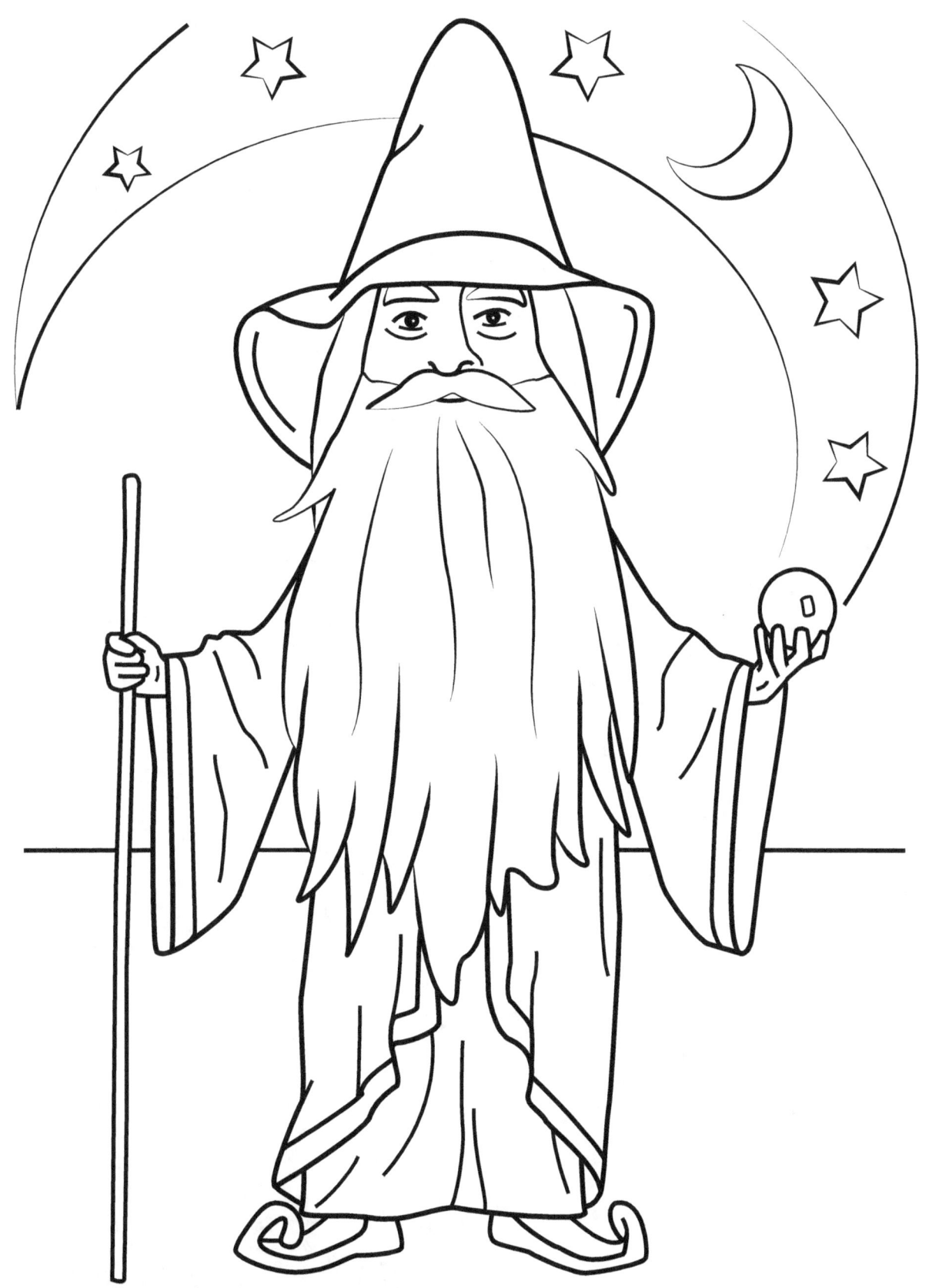

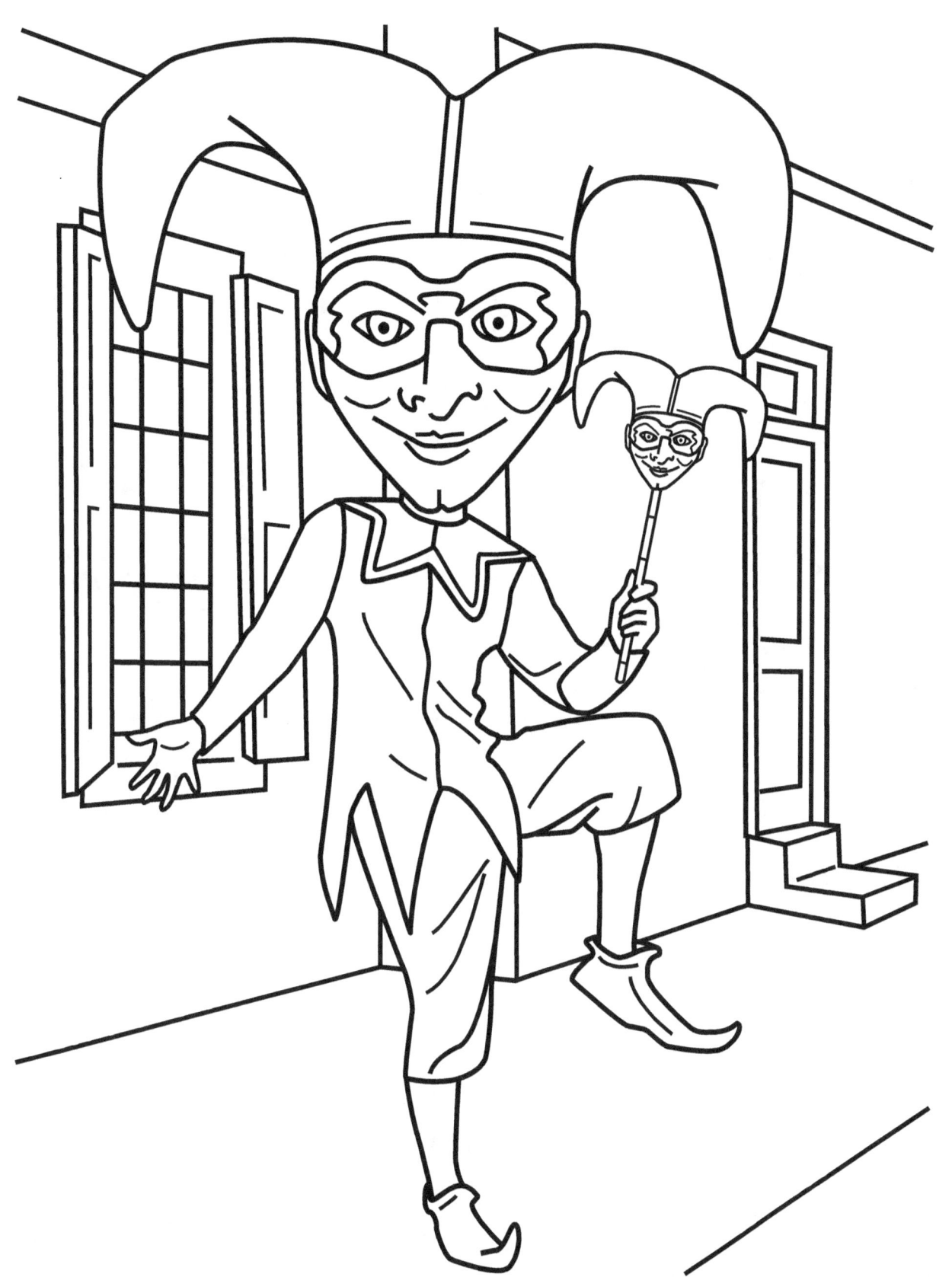

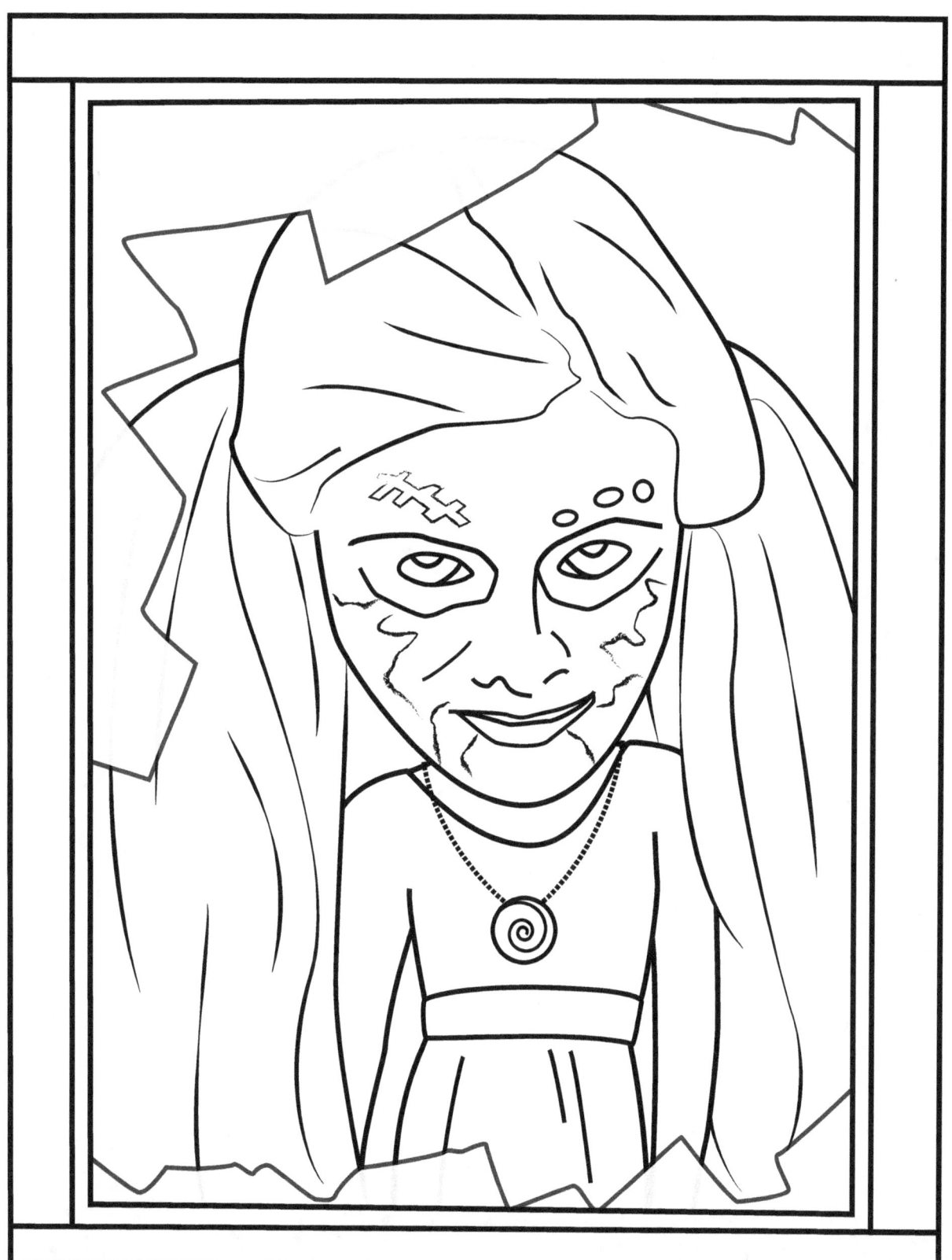

COLOR YOUR OWN

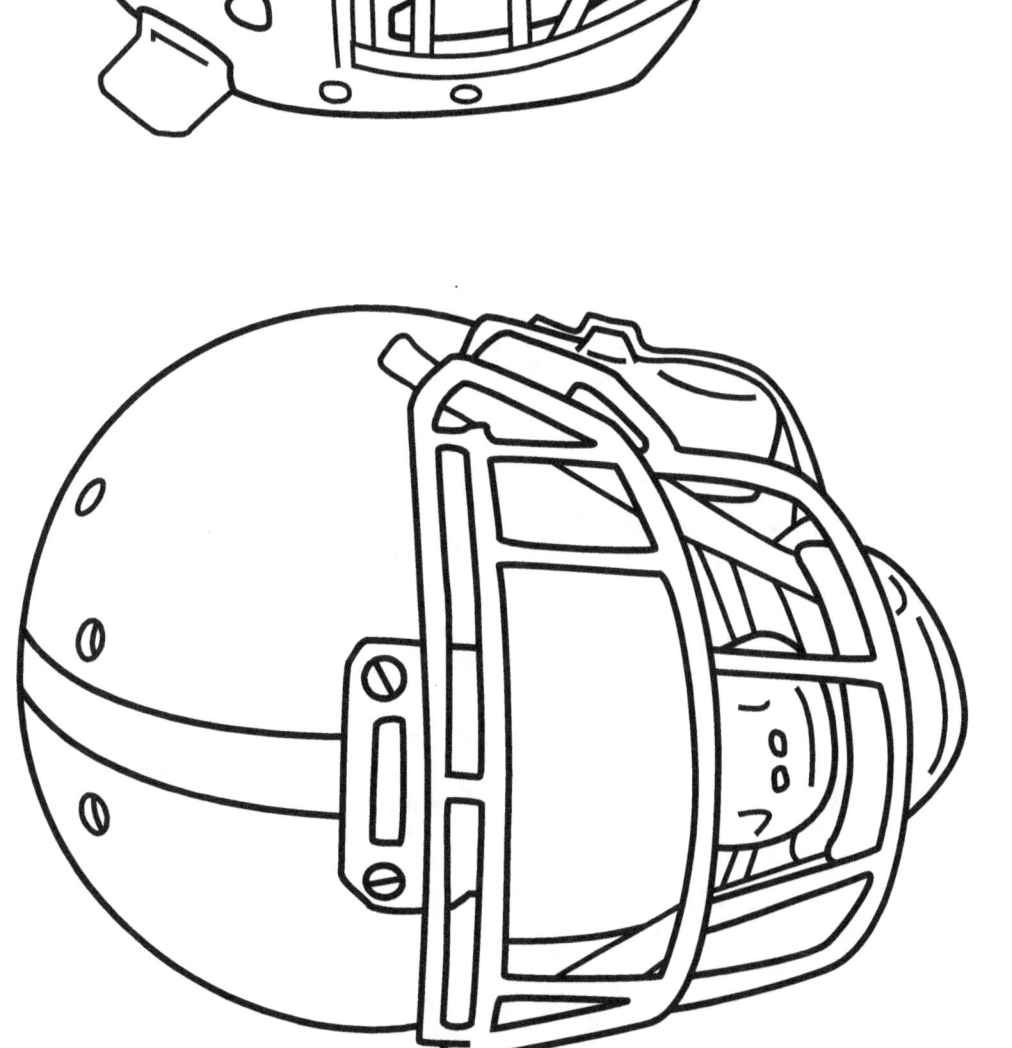

GOALIE MASK

FOOTBALL HELMET

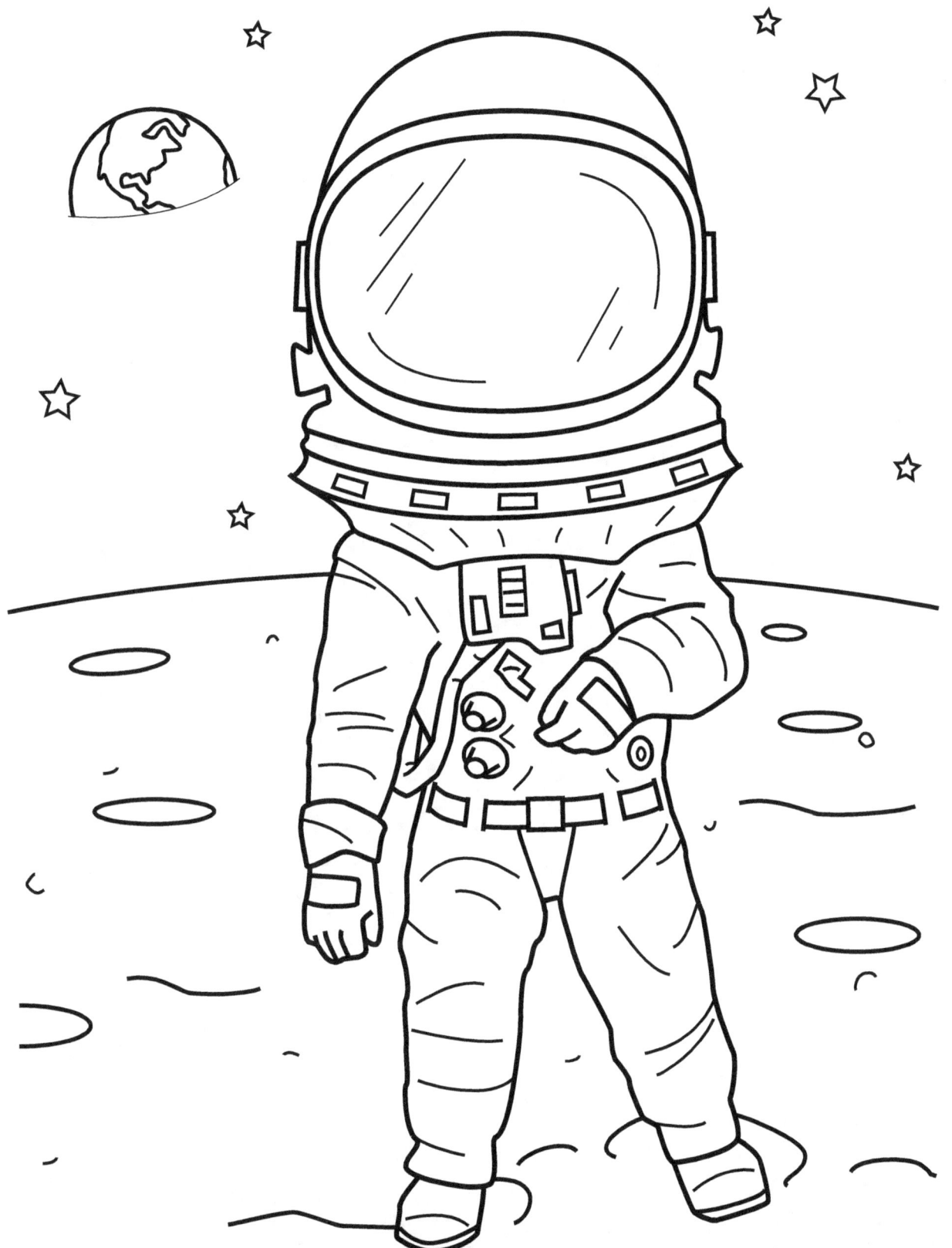

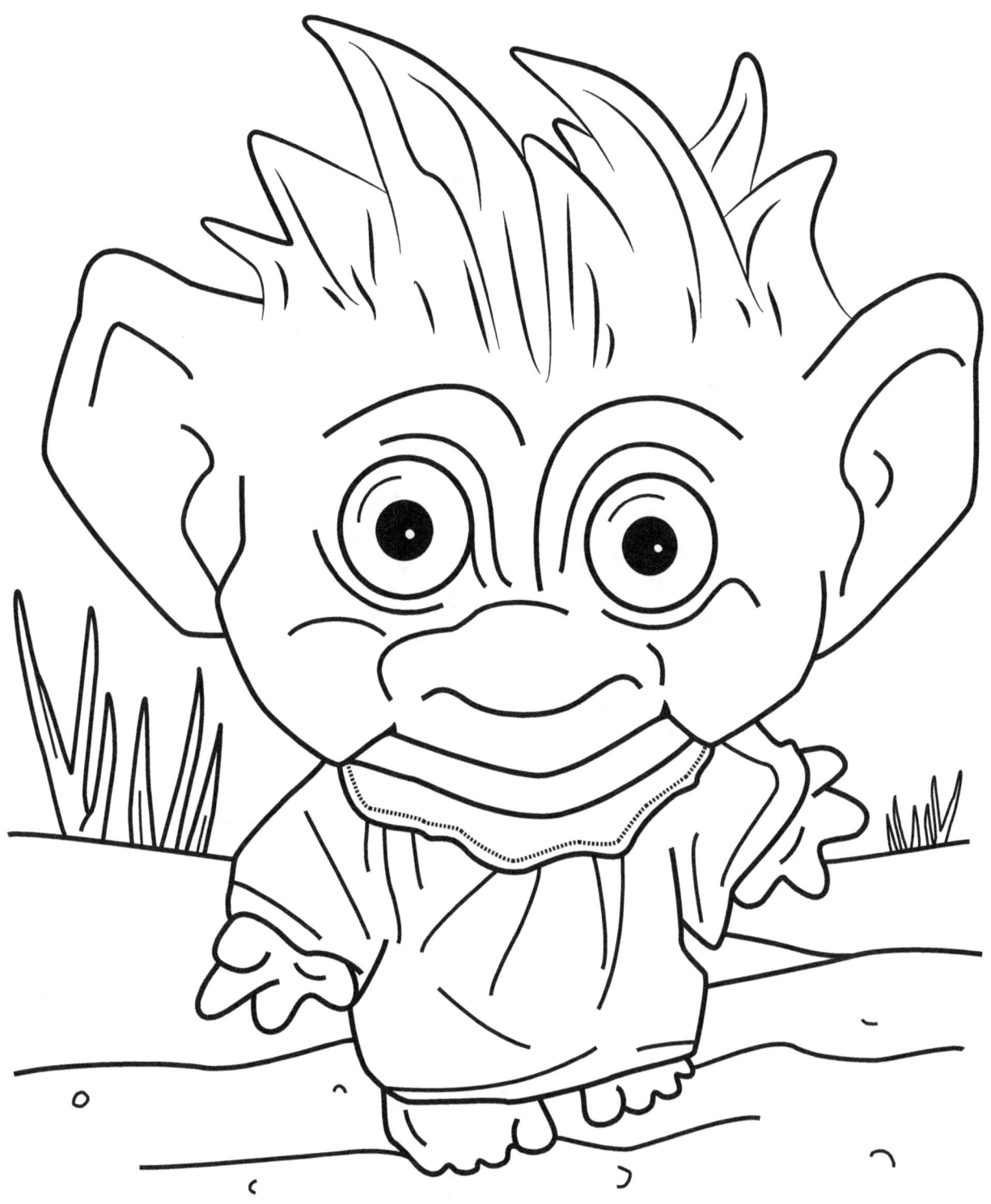

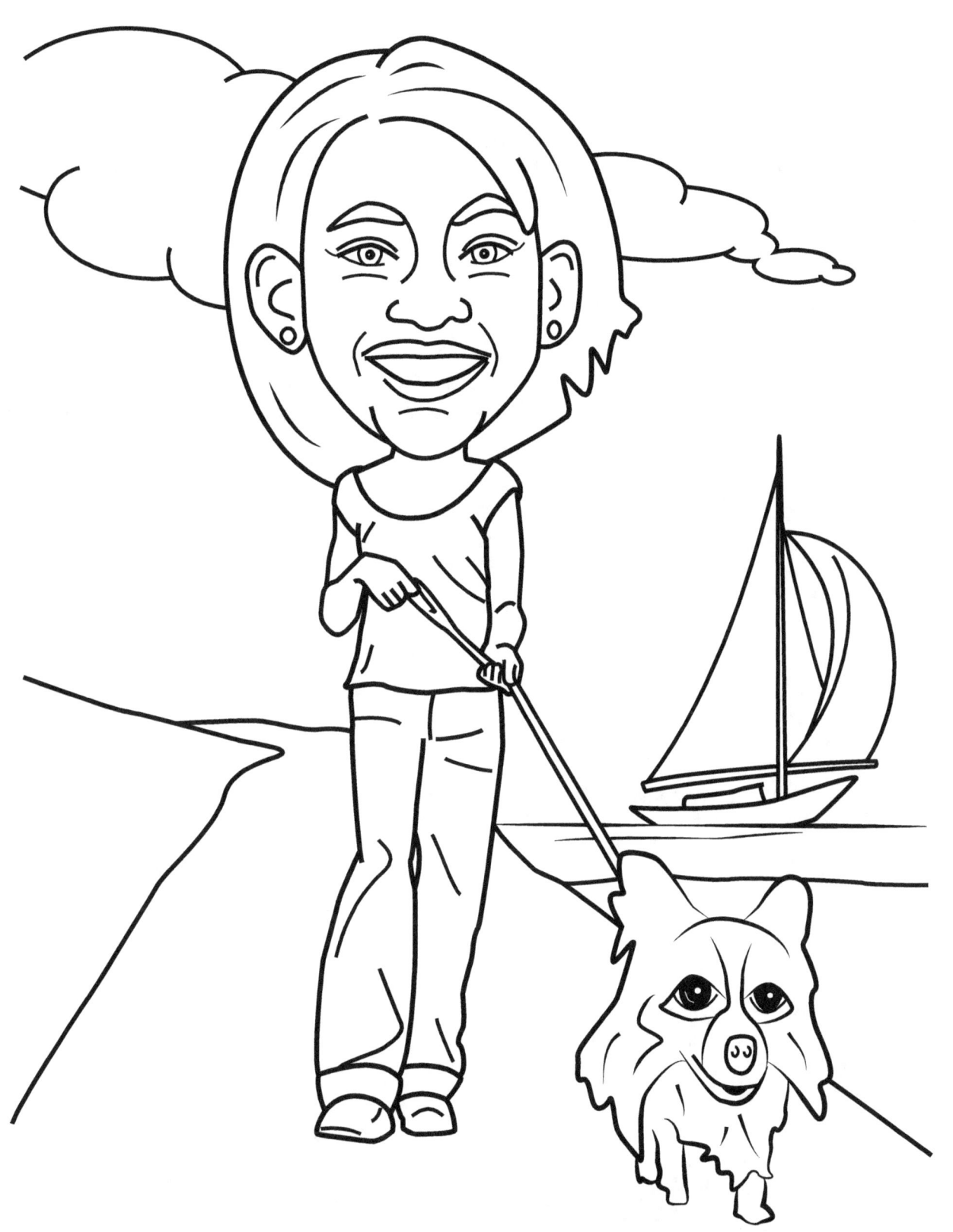

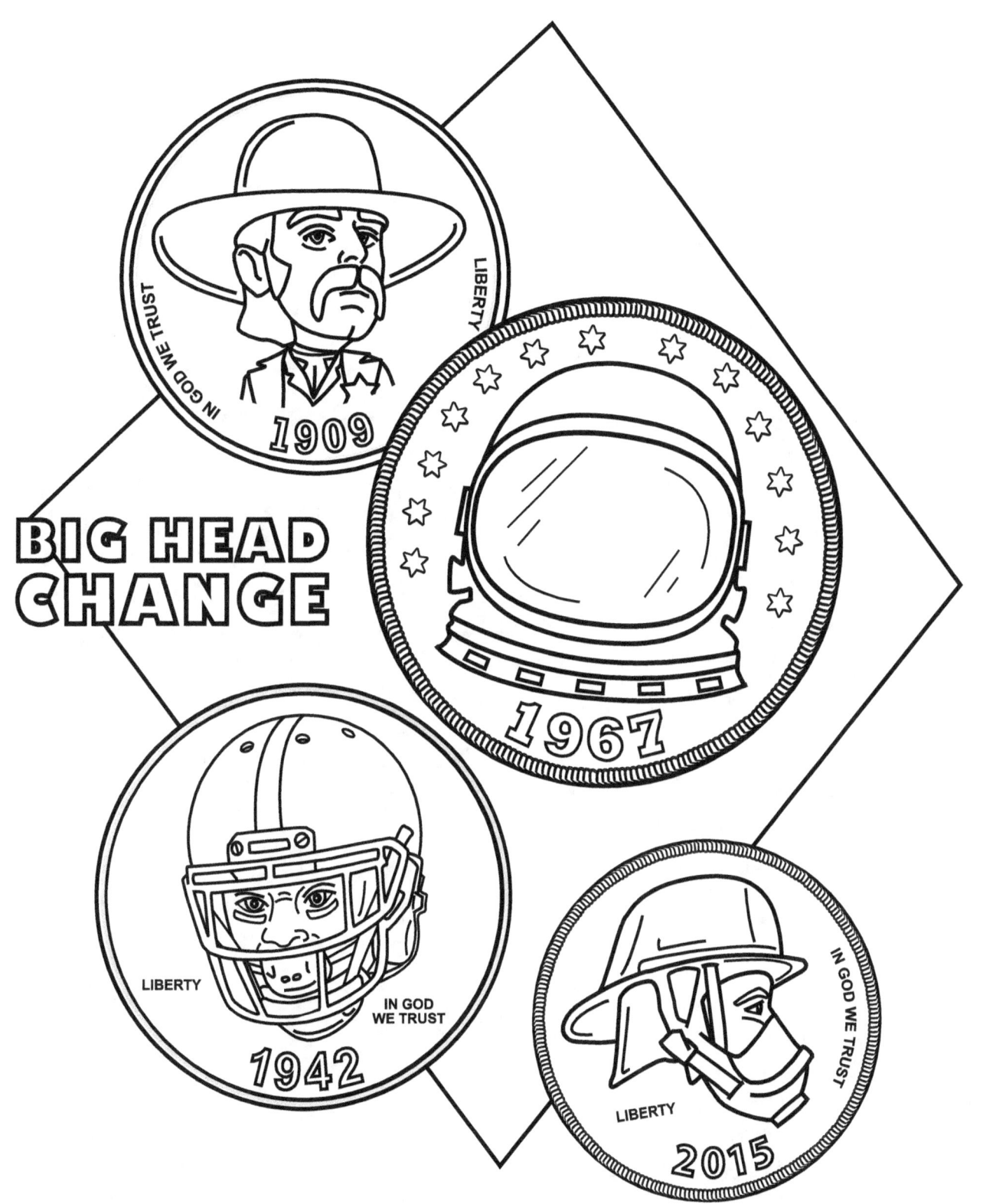

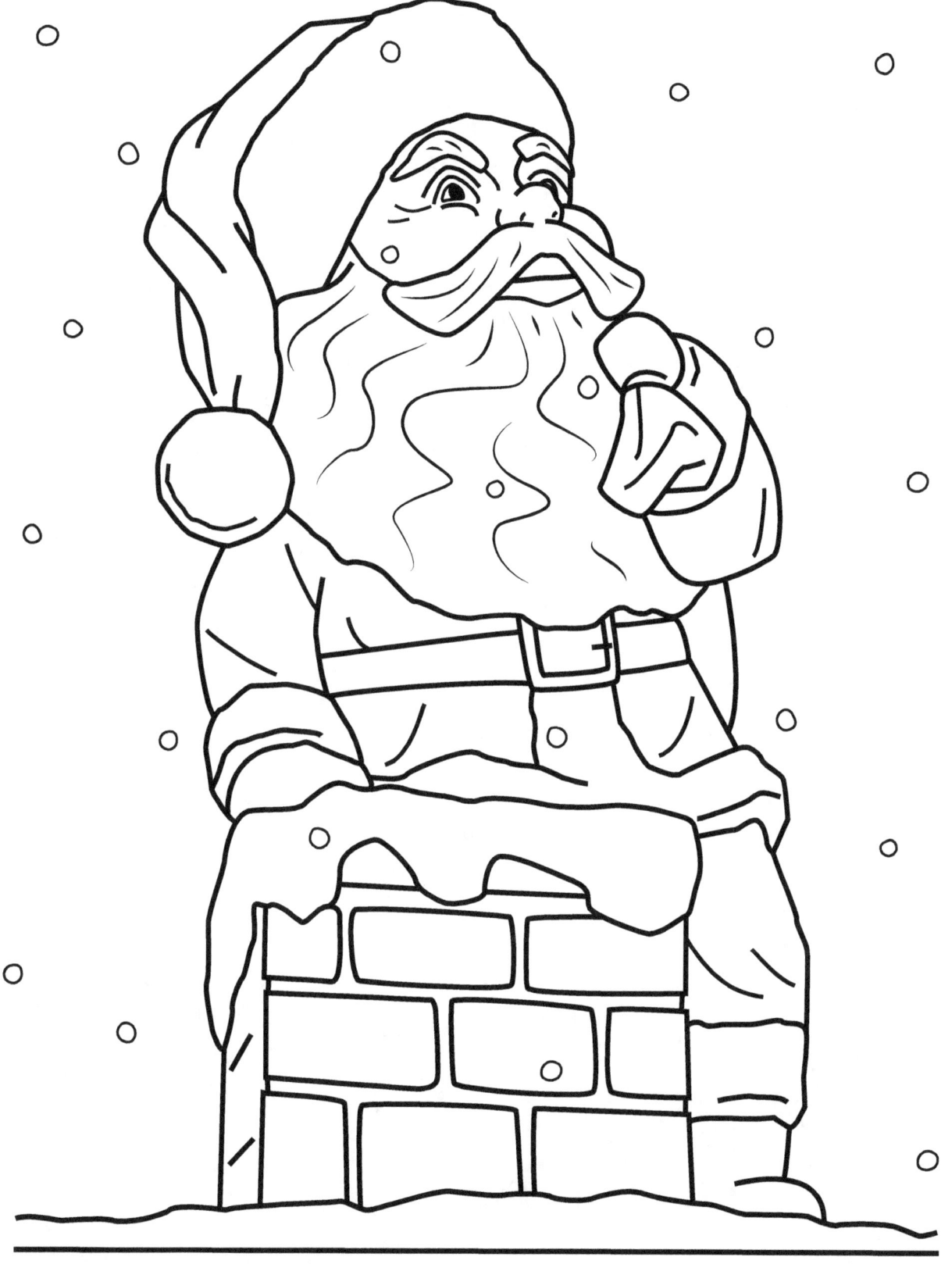

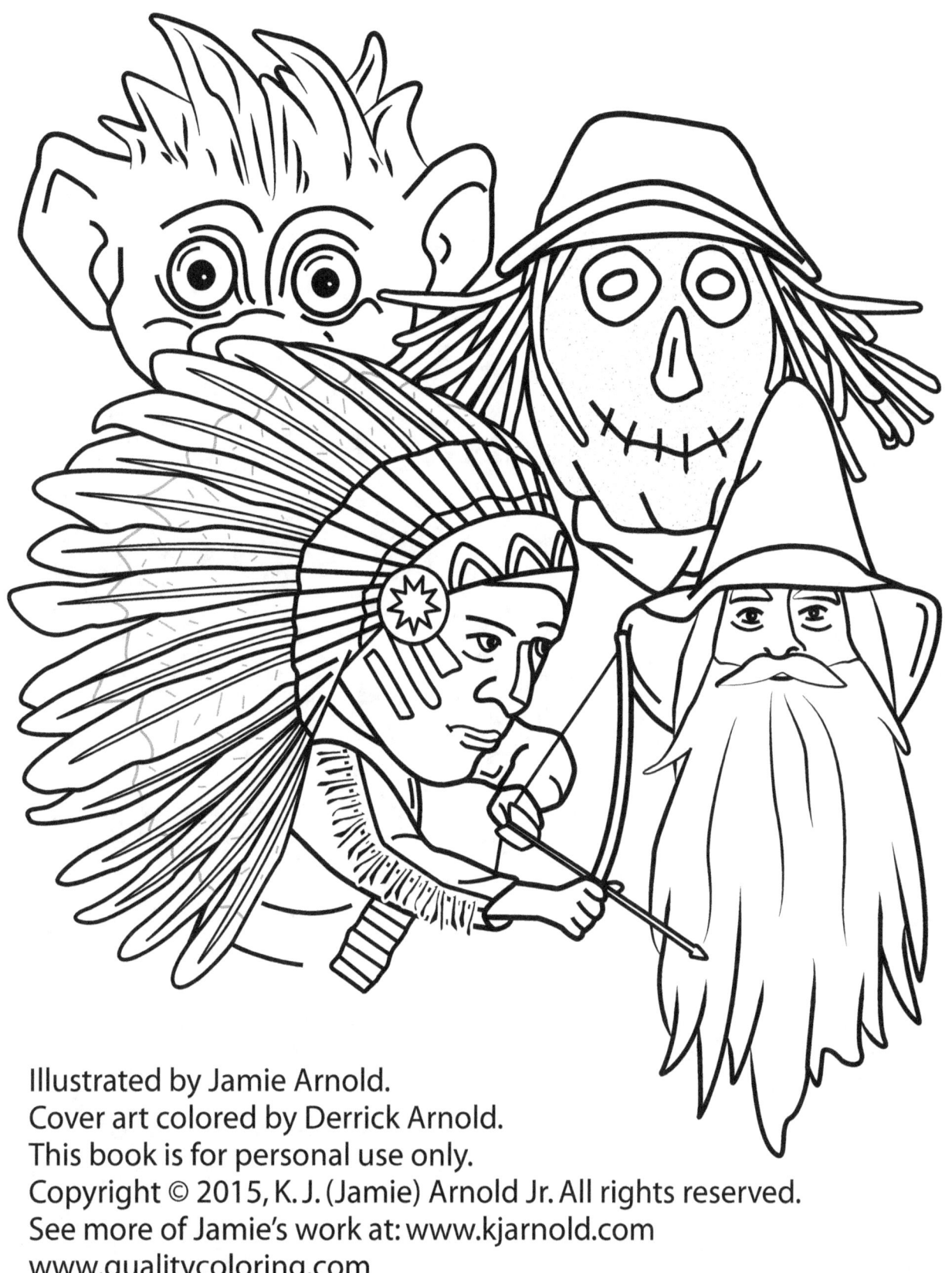

Illustrated by Jamie Arnold.
Cover art colored by Derrick Arnold.
This book is for personal use only.
See more of Jamie's work at: www.kjarnold.com
www.qualitycoloring.com